The Mother I Never Became

Salise M. Haith, an African-American, arrived in London over 20 years ago on a six-month work secondment. Her life took an unexpected turn when she met the man she would marry. Unfortunately, their dream of starting a family through adoption and fertility treatments ended in divorce. Salise believed that children were no longer an option for her.

However, fate intervened when she was assigned to work on a project setting up a new fertility clinic in London. This experience reignited her hope and determination. As a Christian, Salise held onto God's promise for her to have a child, even when it seemed unfulfilled. Through her journey, she discovered something specific that had been blocking that promise.

Today, Salise lives in London and has become a beacon of support for others facing infertility. She is a **Fertility Coach** and the owner of **Lohojo Fertility Support Services**, which stands for the first two letters of Love, Hope, and Joy. Salise empowers women of color, helping them stay resilient and hopeful during the emotional roller coaster of trying to conceive. Her inspiring work includes providing virtual coaching, fertility affirmations calendars, and building a supportive online community.

Salise's story is one of resilience, faith, and compassion, and it continues to impact the lives of many women who share similar struggles.

Instagram: Lohojo.uk

The Mother I Never Became

*One Woman's Story of Surrendering the Dream
to Embrace Divine Validation*

SALISE M. HAITH

*Some names and identifying details have been
changed to protect the privacy of individuals.*

This book is dedicated to everyone who hasn't yet realized she has been living her life for someone else . . . even the child she's hoping for.

And for those who thought that doing everything right would make everything turn out okay.

Contents

Acknowledgements

I want to acknowledge and thank my daddy, the late Malcolm Salis Haith, who was always there for me. I have finally become enlightened to your frequent saying: 'To thine own self be true."

Thank you for your unconditional love.

To my Mum, Beverly Michelle Haith; by accomplishing your dream to write your first book, you have inspired me, so I'm following your lead.

To my three brothers, thank you for always looking after me.

I'm grateful to Pastor Chido Gideon who kept preaching "write the book."

And lastly, I want to thank my precious girlfriends, Miranda Eyles and Sheila Nanka-Bruce. Only heaven can reward you sufficiently for all you have done for me. Thanks for all your unwavering encouragement.

BEGINNING WITH HOPE

An Introduction

The idea to write this book came from my own journey—navigating pain, healing, and eventually finding peace. As I walked through some of the hardest seasons of my life, I went through all this feeling so alone. No one I knew understood how I felt. But years after all the angst of becoming a mature, childless woman, I felt a gentle nudge to write a book about my story. Yet, I was conflicted. I thought, what story is there to write about? A story is supposed to have a fairy-tale ending and that hasn't happened. My story is incomplete, or unfinished. There doesn't seem to be a fairy-tale ending for people who want to have children and a family and don't obtain it.

My hesitation was based on feeling that if a movie doesn't have a good ending—inspirational, hopeful, or good conquering evil—it isn't good. When I told my friend, Donna, I didn't feel comfortable writing a book about my struggles with trying to start a family, she said that people mostly share their happy endings. She pointed out that she rarely hears people talk about stories not having happily-ever-after endings. And that most people talk about their lives as if every obstacle was easily overcome, as if there were no mountains or valleys—just a smooth road to success.

But that's not my story.

My journey has been filled with steep mountains, volcanic ridges, ocean reefs, and desert lands. It's been difficult, yet somehow, I made it through. It may not have been a journey of beautiful scenery, but it was a walk through the wilderness that taught me to let go of idol worship and embrace self-love.

CHAPTER 1

A Change is Coming

A little over a year before my fiftieth birthday, I realized I didn't want my marriage to stay the same. I was about to turn fifty and couldn't imagine spending another decade—or more—caught in this rigmarole, just going through the motions.

I started counselling, knowing that when a relationship feels off, the unhappy partner often has personal issues to work through.

That was me.

I wasn't happy with myself or with how things were at home. Over the next year in therapy, I uncovered many things about my past and upbringing that had shaped me and placed limits on my life. By then, I was ready to let go of those old responsibilities and live more freely.

People look at me and assume I've lived an ideal life. I worked hard to project that image, and from the outside, things do look great. I grew up in a stable, middle-class family, with two supportive parents, a safe neighborhood, good friends, and wonderful experiences. But despite this 'good life,' I still ended up in an unhappy marriage. How did having it all lead me here?

Through therapy, I realized I never truly found my voice. I wasn't the kind of person who would call out friends for their behavior, express anger, or be stubborn to get what I wanted. I grew up thinking that being outspoken or confrontational was something I should avoid.

In many ways, I was sheltered. I never had to worry about much or make decisions for myself. Everything was decided for me: what I would eat, where I could go, what degree I should pursue, even which boyfriends weren't acceptable. I became a people-pleaser from an early age, especially after seeing my parents get upset with my older brother when he didn't follow their rules.

I promised myself I wouldn't make my parents angry—especially my daddy. I didn't want him to be disappointed in me. As a result, I rarely got into trouble and mostly followed the rules.

All the choices my parents made for me limited my ability to make good decisions for myself. Whenever I faced a challenge, I could simply call my daddy, and he was always there to take care of things. I never had to worry. But when it came to choosing boyfriends, I made terrible choices and, of course, I never asked my daddy for advice about them!

I picked those boyfriends because they chose me and seemed nice when they approached me. Living in a well-protected bubble, I assumed everyone was as kind and genuine as I was. I thought people would share my values, enjoy the same things, and want a similar lifestyle, but I couldn't have been more wrong.

My boyfriends in high school and college cheated on me, but I lacked the confidence to stand up for myself and make it clear that cheating was unacceptable.

While I eventually moved on from them, I didn't have the confidence to call them out or say I wouldn't tolerate their behavior. I often stayed longer than I should have, even though my friends could see from the start how wrong they were for me. In some cases, I just put up with it.

They weren't flaunting their cheating, but I knew it was happening—ignored calls, unanswered messages, or friends telling me they'd seen them out with other girls.

It wasn't just happening with boyfriends; I also stayed silent when my boss yelled at me in front of the team, or when I realized I had been underpaid. Instead of asking for a raise, I looked for another job, only to find out that my replacement was given exactly the salary I wanted.

These situations stemmed from the motto I grew up with: If you don't have anything nice to say, don't say anything at all.

As a Southern woman, I was taught to be gracious and polite, to 'keep the peace' and 'not cause a ruckus.' This mindset came from my grandma on my daddy's side. She always tried to keep things peaceful, even during her marriage to her second husband, who treated her poorly. Although my brothers and I disliked him, she would encourage us to greet him, hug him, and engage with him when we visited. We didn't want to, but how could we say no to Grandma?

We were raised to honor and respect our elders, and Grandma deserved our respect for all she had done for our family. It was yet another way I learned to toe the line.

My upbringing shaped how I navigated life. It instilled in me a preference for independence, so I wouldn't have to cater to anyone else or justify my choices when I wanted things my way.

These were just some of the insights I uncovered in therapy before my divorce. Yet, even after a year of therapy, I still struggled to love, appreciate, or advocate for myself. Although I came to understand myself more deeply, I wasn't ready to make changes in my relationship.

I'd grown comfortable in my marriage. Despite the challenges, I didn't want a divorce; I wanted a happy-ever-after, even after so much had gone wrong.

When Julian, and I got married, I genuinely wanted our relationship to succeed. I had witnessed both strong and struggling marriages and was determined to avoid the pitfalls I'd seen.

At our wedding, I put out a table with note cards, pens, and a sign inviting guests to share their marriage advice. Without any pre-marital counselling, I felt gathering others' wisdom might help us build a lasting, happy marriage. I didn't doubt we could make it work, but I knew it would require effort, and I welcomed any insights that could guide us.

To my disappointment, the advice was underwhelming. Most cards simply read things like, 'Don't go to bed angry' and 'Be nice to each other.' This early in our relationship, these seemed like manageable basics, not the deeper guidance I was hoping for to sustain a lifetime together.

CHAPTER 2

The Discovery of Mr. Right

Julian* and I met a few months after I came to London from America, at an African and Caribbean networking event. His best friend and I worked at the same consulting firm, and, as I later found out, Julian had been persistently prompting him to introduce us.

When we were introduced, I first noticed Julian was a tall, large man with fair skin and a warm northern British accent. He smiled and asked, "Where are you from?"

"I'm from North Carolina, but I live in Chicago," I replied.

He asked about my being in London, and I said, "I'm here for work on a secondment."

After more small talk, with a curious expression, he asked, "Do you like Oprah?"

I was caught off guard, thinking, 'Why is this big man asking me if I like Oprah?'

But I answered, "Of course, I like Oprah—who doesn't?"

With a smirk, he clarified, "I didn't say Oprah, I said opera."

I laughed at myself, realizing the faux pas, and Julian laughed with me. He then asked if I'd be interested in going to the Royal Opera House to see an opera.

I was impressed. "Yes, but it would depend on whether my work's month-end activities are finished in time."

I asked him to follow up closer to the date. After exchanging numbers and chatting a bit more, I thought he seemed like a nice man who genuinely wanted to connect over things I enjoyed. Over the next few weeks, we spoke on the phone and got to know each other better before our date.

The evening of our first date I made another faux pas. We agreed to meet at Covent Garden in London, and as I came out of the tube station, I spotted Julian standing near a Tiffany & Co. jewelry store. He smiled warmly at me as I walked over, and when I stretched out my arms to give him a hug, he leaned in with his lips pursed. Startled, I pulled back.

He chuckled and said, "I was trying to give you a kiss on both cheeks. That's what we do over here."

I laughed nervously, thinking, 'Oh, my goodness, I've messed up again!' But Julian was gracious. He gave me a kiss on both cheeks, and we went on to enjoy the opera. The performance was incredible—the vocals were stunning—but I was even more impressed to learn that Julian's sister had a role in the production. That thoughtful and cultured first date left me intrigued and wanting to know more about him.

After our date, Julian insisted on driving me home since it was late. I agreed, feeling confident in my sense of direction and knowing his best friend worked with me. However, navigating the streets of London threw me completely—I had no idea where we were going. Julian mentioned he needed to use the restroom and said he would stop by his house, assuring me it wasn't far from where we were.

As we drove, I stared out the window, trying to memorize landmarks in case I needed to retrace my steps. When we arrived at his house, I said I'd stay in the car, but he encouraged me to come inside and meet his mother. Reluctantly, I agreed.

Inside, Julian introduced me to his mother, a lovely, petite woman with a slight Jamaican accent. She greeted me warmly and asked where I was from and how long I'd be in London. I replied, "I'm from North Carolina, and I'm here on a six-month work assignment."

Just as the conversation was picking up, Julian returned and said it was time to leave. Whew, that was a relief! We weren't at the stage to meet his family. I had just met him, but I think he was just getting her to give me a once-over without him around.

Back in the car, he drove me home, and we talked about the differences between life in the UK and the US. Julian shared stories about his work travels and mentioned he had been to the US several times and had family there. He had also travelled extensively for work, including working in Australia. I was impressed as I knew there was more of the world that I'd like to see. It was an easy, engaging conversation that made the drive fly by. But then, he mentioned something peculiar, which made me feel like I understood why he wanted me to meet his mother. Years earlier, he and his youngest sister had seen a psychic, who predicted he'd marry a foreigner with blue eyes. He did not outright say that he thought that person was me, but I wanted to know more and asked him about it. How long ago did this happen? Where did you see the psychic? He was fuzzy with the details. He couldn't remember when they saw her. He remembered that his sister wanted to visit the psychic, and he went along. But it was too early for predictions. I barely knew if I liked the man.

I stored that story in the back of my mind to question again in the future if this was confirmation that this was the man I would marry. Even though I knew psychics were on the dark side, I felt like there was a possibility of truth to what he said because I believed they could see the future. Obviously, she was able to see me in Julian's timeline.

As he drove me home, I stared out the window, unsure whether to feel flattered, chosen, or just quietly unnerved. I watched the city pass by, caught somewhere between curiosity and a quiet sense of unease. By the time he dropped me off, I felt like I had gotten to know another side of him—someone worldly, thoughtful, and kind.

Our first date went well, and we continued to see each other. We went out for dinners and drinks after work and spent weekends together, enjoying each other's company and getting to know one another better.

Julian was educated in the UK, had travelled extensively, and held a respectable job working in IT. He had a good circle of friends and a strong relationship with his family. He was a nice, funny, and intelligent man who was also thoughtful. He put effort into planning fun and engaging dates, and we genuinely enjoyed spending time together. It felt easy and natural, and our connection deepened as the weeks went by.

We dated for several months, and everything seemed to be going smoothly, but I started to question whether I should be with him. Julian was nice, but something just didn't feel right. I couldn't pinpoint what it was, but I couldn't shake the feeling.

One evening, I decided to call him. After some small talk, I hesitated before saying, "I think we should break up." He was surprised and asked, "But why?"

"I don't think we're compatible. We don't have a lot in common."

We didn't like the same types of books to read, I liked city break holidays, he liked being at home doing nothing. I wanted to take holidays. He didn't. He enjoyed binge-watching television series. I would rather be out exploring the world.

Julian disagreed. He told me he didn't want us to break up and asked me to reconsider. "Let's just continue to go out and see where this goes."

Reluctantly, I agreed. Part of me was thinking about what so many people had told me before I moved to London: "You're going to meet your husband over there!" Was Julian the one? I didn't know.

I kept questioning things until one day we visited his best friend, where I met his wife and their two children. Julian was their children's godfather, and that struck me. I had never heard of a single man being entrusted with such a responsibility.

Finding out that Julian was a godfather was the thing that tipped the scale for me. It signaled a kind of reliability and warmth I hadn't expected. It made me see him differently—like maybe he wasn't just fun and charming—but someone people trusted with something meaningful. That moment made me pause and seriously consider a future with him. It gave me a sense of reassurance, as though maybe this was someone I could build something with.

From that point on, we continued dating, and our feelings for each other grew stronger. I started to feel more certain about him, thinking he really could be the one.

One day, Julian asked me if I would move in with him. I was taken aback. Was he serious?

I immediately told him, "No, I'm not moving in with someone who lives abroad, and we're not married."

In my mind, the idea was completely out of the question. I thought, "I'm not living with anyone who could just kick me out of their house, leaving me homeless in a foreign country. Absolutely not."

But that conversation made it clear that our relationship was becoming more serious. We were spending more and more time together, and I started to realize that Julian saw a future for us which I was now happy with as well.

I decided to compare Julian to my 'husband checklist.' I didn't just have a checklist—I had an Excel spreadsheet. Properly set up, with headings and columns, about 20 qualities I wanted in 'the one' and even a few names of past partners entered in for comparison. It might sound clinical, but it helped me be honest with myself about what I needed in a relationship—and what hadn't worked before. So, when things with Julian started getting serious, I added him to the list. And to my surprise, he matched nearly every quality

I was looking for. The only mark against him was that he smoked. But honestly, it didn't bother me as much as I thought it might. He never smoked indoors, his house didn't smell, and neither did he. It wasn't ideal, but it also wasn't a deal breaker.

We were in love, getting along wonderfully, and everything felt like it was falling into place. Two years after coming to London on a work secondment, Julian and I got married, and I relocated to London permanently to start our life together.

CHAPTER 3

Get on the Baby Train

Julian and I had only been married a few months when he said, "I think we should adopt." I frowned, thinking, 'Why would you say that? We haven't even started trying to have a family.'

We had already agreed that we both wanted children and had planned to enjoy our first year of marriage, getting to know each other better, before starting a family. Having children was one of the reasons we felt compatible as a couple, so I brushed off his comment. Little did I know that statement would come back to haunt me years later.

After our first year of marriage, I didn't feel any urgency to start a family, so we simply continued enjoying life as it was—dining out, cozy nights in, traveling abroad to see my family in the States, and visiting his parents and siblings here in the UK on weekends. We relished living the carefree 'life of Riley,' with no immediate responsibilities or set timeline for having children.

But as our closest friends began to get married and start families, I felt a shift. Suddenly, I realized we were falling behind in a way I hadn't anticipated; while we'd once been ahead, it now seemed like it was time to get on the baby train.

I didn't think much about trying to get pregnant—I assumed that if we had sex regularly, it would eventually happen. But after nearly a year with no results, I started to worry, especially as more of my friends announced their pregnancies.

Determined to understand what was going on, I began researching how to conceive. I re-learned the basics of reproduction and was surprised to discover that conception is only possible a few days each month. All those years of careful birth control, and now I couldn't get pregnant. It was bewildering.

It became a deeply painful time for me. Night after night, I cried myself to sleep, struggling with feelings of frustration, shame, jealousy, and grief over unfulfilled dreams. Not being able to conceive took a toll on our marriage. I'm sure Julian felt isolated by the weight of my need for his sperm, as I was primarily focused on conceiving, adding strain to our relationship. Nothing else was as important as our regular intervals of intimacy. Yet, each month brought fresh disappointment, leaving us both heartbroken and exhausted.

After two years of trying, during our fourth year of marriage, we finally decided to see a doctor. After assessing our reproductive health and reviewing our medical history, she quickly placed us on the council-funded waiting list for fertility treatment. We resumed our routine, unaware of how long the wait would be, or our position on the list.

Over a year later, we reached the top and scheduled our first appointment in November.

Julian and I didn't discuss at length what fertility treatment might be like or how it might affect us emotionally. We simply went through the recommended tests and scans. They advised us to have the intracytoplasmic sperm injection (ICSI) treatment. We agreed—it seemed like the best option—and we didn't know of any alternatives. We were moving forward toward having a family, but I sensed neither of us felt excited or close to one another. We had already been disconnected for some time, and the weight of knowing this could be our only chance was daunting. After so much disappointment, feeling hopeful was difficult.

We each handled the stress in our own way. I was willing to do whatever it took to make the treatment successful. Julian, however, seemed overwhelmed, as though he wanted the pressure to be lifted from him. The stress must have been immense; he was going out after work more, drinking and smoking. I could sense his anxiety about what this meant for our relationship, as he likely struggled with feelings of helplessness, frustration, and the burden of constant disappointment. I only knew to nag him to stop drinking and smoking, but he didn't. Was it self-sabotage? Was this too much pressure for him? He wouldn't discuss it with me. Regardless of our personal struggles, nothing was going to stop us and we proceeded with starting our fertility treatment.

To prepare for the egg retrieval, I had to give myself daily hormone injections to stimulate my ovaries, helping the follicles mature the eggs for collection. These eggs would then be fertilized with Julian's sperm to create zygotes.

I visited the clinic frequently for ultrasounds to monitor the effects of the medications. The nurse would pour cold gel on my stomach and press the ultrasound around to see if the medication was working effectively to mature the eggs in my follicles. As I lay on the table looking at the monitor, I would imagine a future ultrasound appointment detecting a growing baby instead of maturing follicles. At that moment, I had hope that the family I wanted might soon happen. I had no idea how many eggs might have matured, but the sonographer reassured me that the medication was working well.

On the day of my egg retrieval in March, they successfully collected over fifteen eggs. Julian made his sperm donation that same day, and we were set for the ICSI procedure. Afterwards, they sent us home and scheduled our embryo transfer appointment for the following week. For those five days, we held onto hope, imagining the embryos growing, though we'd have to wait until the appointment to know for sure.

At our next appointment for the embryo transfer, our doctor informed us that, unfortunately, most zygotes hadn't developed into embryos, but two had, and she was satisfied with those results. She told us she had selected these two embryos to be transferred. We were thrilled to proceed, and after she completed the transfer, I was officially pregnant!

Surprisingly, the procedure was quick and uneventful. It took less than 20 minutes—getting undressed seemed to take longer. Julian later confessed that he felt unnerved seeing me talk to him and the doctor one moment, only to fall asleep under sedation the next moment while I was just talking to him. But when I came around, that was it. All the hard work and preparation had led us to this moment: we were now pregnant, hoping this would finally lead to parenthood.

Yet, even in this moment, neither of us felt particularly optimistic. After five years of monthly disappointment, we'd learned to temper our expectations. Despite the excitement of this step, we were cautious, as the journey so far had taught us how fragile hope could be.

After the procedure, the doctor advised me to go home and carry on as usual. But once we got home, I went to take a nap, propping a pillow under my hips. This was one of the tips I had read online to give myself the best chance for implantation. I fell asleep quickly. When I woke up, there was nothing more I could do but wait—the infamous two-week wait. Two long weeks until I could take a pregnancy test and find out if the embryos had implanted in my womb and I was going to have a baby.

Each day, my mind was filled with questions: What's happening inside me? Is a baby growing? Will it stay? Should I be feeling anything? Are my breasts more tender? Could that twinge or cramp be implantation? Will I finally become the mother I've dreamed of being? Will having a child make Julian and I happier? Will this child change everything for us? Does Julian even want this as much as I do? Will this bring us closer or strain our relationship even more?

Every possible thought and worry ran through my mind, yet deep down, I wasn't convinced it would happen. I had a hope but not a conviction. Something felt off. This wasn't how it was supposed to be. We were supposed to be excited, and planning for the future. Getting closer. Looking to get prams, and having our parents be grandparents. Nothing was changing. The drift between Julian and I was not closing, and we certainly weren't discussing our hopes of becoming parents or our dreams of raising a happy, healthy child. But none of that mattered now; all I could do was wait and see.

Finally, the day arrived. The long two-week wait after the embryo transfer was over. That morning, I woke up, turned over and looked at Julian. The sun was shining, and the morning breeze stirred the curtains. He was already awake. We just looked at each other knowing today we'd find out if I was pregnant. I hesitated to get out of bed and take the pregnancy test, but he encouraged me to go ahead. I touched my stomach. Was I feeling anything down there? I went to the bathroom and opened yet another pregnancy test. I wished I had been investing in these Clearblue stocks all this time. I would be rich. I peed on the stick and sat it carefully on the side of the sink, looking to see the first line appear. I didn't want to watch for the second line so returned to bed to wait. Those five minutes dragged by painfully slow. Julian set the timer on his phone for five minutes. When the alarm rang, I went to check the result, and there it was again. That same mountain of my life that I continually walked around . . . disappointment.

The test read 'Not Pregnant.'

I showed Julian the pregnancy test and told him again, "I'm not pregnant." We were both crushed, but we didn't talk about it, console each other, or even cry. We just sat in silence. It was heartbreaking and deeply painful to mentally prepare to call everyone who'd been hoping for good news and tell them we weren't pregnant. Especially since everyone expected the best outcome.

As we called our parents and then our friends, their kind words of "You can try again" or "It'll happen for you" brought no real comfort. While we appreciated their support, we felt so deeply these losses of not being a mother, not having family Christmas photos, or seeing our children in their school uniforms. Failing this attempt at parenthood left a gaping pain that lingered, making us question our worth and deepening our sense of failure.

After years of trying, knowing this was our one shot, the disappointment hit even harder. I had to summon the strength to call the clinic and report the outcome, feeling the weight of so many unanswered questions. Why hadn't the embryo implanted? Was it the quality of my eggs? Julian's sperm? His diabetes? My past abortion? My lack of faith? His drinking or smoking? Each reason seemed possible, yet we knew other couples who had conceived in similar circumstances. I called and left a message for the nurse to call me back. When she did, I told her my test was negative. She gave me her condolences and I began asking her the questions.

"Do you know why I didn't get pregnant?"

She said she didn't know.

I knew asking her further questions would bring no clarity, so I gave her the information she needed, and we ended the call.

On top of it all, we didn't have the funds for another cycle, nor did we realize that successful pregnancies often require multiple fertility treatments. I did not have any answers and was content when we didn't immediately discuss any of it.

A few weeks later, Julian asked if I wanted to try again, but I was firm in my decision not to. After the egg retrieval, I had developed ovarian hyperstimulation syndrome (OHSS), a rare and dangerous side effect of the hormone treatments, which had put my life at risk. I couldn't go through that ordeal again. I wasn't going to die just to have a baby.

Plus, I also felt resentment building. I believed Julian could have done more to prepare himself: quitting smoking, eating better, losing weight, and exercising well before our treatment. His self-sabotaging habits, combined with the disappointing outcome, created further distance between us. I was mad and blamed him. He dealt with it by shutting down, avoiding any conversation about the process, or his role in it. I imagine he didn't want to face my disappointment or hear my concerns about how his choices were affecting our chance to have a family. Behind this avoidance, though, I sensed he carried feelings of guilt and responsibility. I knew he was aware that his health issues were contributing factors, and I imagined he felt isolated, despite having supportive friends. With his sense of masculinity at stake, it must have been challenging for him to express his emotions to me, perhaps fearing I would see him differently or think less of him as a partner.

CHAPTER 4

Have You Considered Adoption?

Four years after our failed fertility treatment, another opportunity to build our family appeared when Julian suggested we consider adoption. I thought, 'Hmm, that's a different option. Maybe that could work?'

A couple of days later, I spotted an adoption flyer and asked him, "Do you want to go?"

"Yes," he said, and I considered it a sign.

I didn't register for the adoption event right away. I was still mulling over whether this was truly the path I wanted to take. I thought back to those early days in our marriage when Julian first mentioned adoption. Maybe now was the time, and this was the way we were meant to build our family. But I hesitated. I wasn't sure if our marriage was strong enough to support the journey of raising an adopted child.

A week later, a colleague asked me if I knew of any church with a baptismal pool. I did and recalled a woman who adopted her daughter whose church had a baptismal pool. I felt this was another sign. I didn't immediately get in contact, but a couple of weeks later, I decided to email her. My email said:

'I think my thinking of you is God's way of getting me to talk to you about adopting. After nine years, Julian and I haven't had our own yet. But I had a dream the other day of my pastor telling me to go get my child from Ireland. So, do you mind giving me your number and letting me know if you'd be interested in talking to me about the process?'

She responded positively to my email. Although I was hesitant, it took me another couple of weeks to call her. When I finally did, we talked for a couple of hours. She shared her entire adoption journey with me. She was thrilled with how it had gone and had been enjoying life with her daughter, who had been with her for six months. After hearing her positive experience, I asked for the details of the adoption agency she used, as she gave them such glowing reviews. For the first time, I felt a bit of hope about this possibility.

Shortly after, I saw a flyer for an information session organized by the adoption agency my friend had recommended. It felt too serendipitous to ignore, like the final sign pushing me to move forward. I went home and asked Julian if he'd like to attend, and he agreed. So, I registered for the session.

The following week, we arrived at the adoption information event. As we approached the registration desk, the social workers greeted us with noticeable excitement, which surprised me. Looking back, I realized we must have appeared as an ideal candidate couple. Perhaps they could already picture a child in our arms, though I knew it was too early to think that way. We were still aware of the challenges that can come with the adoption approval process.

The session began with the social workers welcoming everyone and explaining the steps involved: meeting with caseworkers, delving into our family history, and ultimately having an assessment report prepared with a recommendation for the adoption panel. We then heard from a single woman who shared her successful adoption journey, which was incredibly encouraging.

The agency also shared those previous restrictions—such as marital status, sexual orientation, or housing—were no longer barriers. As a married, heterosexual Black couple, we didn't face any of those constraints. Julian and I discussed it on the way home and felt confident in moving forward with the process.

It took about six weeks for our adoption process to really begin, starting with an initial interview with a social worker at the adoption agency in Chelsea. We met with several social workers there over a few weeks and were given lots of paperwork to complete. Applications forms, employment history, medical history and more. After wading through mountains of paperwork, we entered months of rigorous background checks and home visits designed to assess us on every level including our resilience towards loss, and our ability to care for a child or children with traumatic pasts. We met with various social workers until finally being assigned a dedicated one, Sandra. She was kind and shared our cultural background, yet she didn't hold back in identifying areas where she felt we needed to grow to be "good enough" parents, as they put it.

Sandra was direct, probing into every aspect of our lives: our finances, our intimacy, how we handled conflict, our childhoods, our parents' relationships, and even if we'd ever considered leaving each other. These sessions were uncomfortable and unsettling. I'd never discussed these things so openly. It felt as if she was unlocking a part of me that I had long kept hidden.

It reminded me of the curio cabinet in my grandma's dining room. Inside were her most treasured possessions: delicate porcelain figurines, gold-rimmed glassware, antique tea sets, and crystal candy dishes filled with handwritten notes and tucked-away money. These items were only to be admired from a distance, safely locked away behind glass. It felt like Sandra had found the key to my own internal curio cabinet, opened it, and was intent on exploring every hidden piece. Every week, she'd pick up one item, ask me about it, and before I could put it back, she was pulling out another to examine. All my carefully arranged 'collectibles' were exposed, scattered outside their protective case. I was emotionally raw, feeling that every neatly compartmentalized piece of my life had been disrupted.

I hadn't realized just how much I'd compartmentalized my life—each issue locked away, available only for quick glances but never full inspection. I hadn't expected the process to be so invasive, and it felt as though a whirlwind had swept through my life, leaving nothing of my comfort intact.

During our adoption interview sessions, we were asked to share our most profound life experiences, particularly from our childhoods. Discussing these memories was challenging, often triggering emotions we hadn't revisited in years.

It was hard to dive into these details with the social worker, but we managed to get through it.

Surprisingly, Julian and I learned things about each other's childhoods that we had never discussed before and probably would have never known outside of this experience.

On top of recognizing my own emotional issues of mother wounds, I was frustrated to realize that our relationship wasn't as strong as I felt it needed to be.

I thought, 'What am I doing? How can I bring a child into this home when we struggle to discuss our own issues, let alone the needs of a child?'

I worried about how we'd handle the challenges of parenting an adopted child. What if the child required extra attention? What if they played us against each other? How could we work as a team when we could barely have a good conversation ourselves?

I dreaded the thought of putting everything into raising this child, only for our marriage to break down and create more trauma for them. I was expecting huge changes in Julian's lifestyle. I wanted him to be more physically fit, to quit smoking and drinking, and for us to be better connected emotionally. And at various points in our relationship, he had been working with a personal trainer, had quit smoking, and we were closely connected, but not at the times when it mattered the most.

Even though we were moving forward, deep down, I knew our relationship was faltering and that we lacked the solid foundation needed for success. Yet, we were approved to adopt. It was bittersweet, knowing that although many couples face similar issues and still have children, our unresolved struggles added complexity to an already challenging journey.

One major hurdle was that Julian and I weren't aligned on the age of the child we wanted. He preferred an older child, hoping to avoid diaper changes and midnight feedings. I, on the other hand, wanted the youngest child possible, hoping to reduce the impact of early neglect or trauma and give us a chance to shape their experience from a young age. We didn't come to a resolution on this. With each child that came through the system, our social worker and the baby finder would ask, "What do you think of this one?" but our differing visions created an ongoing tension.

They sent us profiles of children of every age and background. We'd look at their smiling faces, read about them, but we couldn't decide on any because we lacked a shared vision. Each time a profile arrived, I'd say, "What about this one?" and Julian would say, "Nope." And we would look at the next profile and he'd ask, "How about this one?" and I'd say, "Nope."

We weren't on the same page. Whether boys or girls, younger or older, even siblings—demographics didn't matter so much as the tragic stories of neglect and trauma. Many had backgrounds involving maternal drug use, abandonment, or abuse. Reflecting on it now, I'm horrified by how many vulnerable children we had to choose from.

Then we saw the profile of two adorable brothers with warm brown skin, much like Julian's, and thought they might be a good match. Finally, we agreed and told the social workers we were interested in moving forward. It was both exciting and terrifying. What were we in for? Their social worker arranged a visit to our home, and I started feeling hopeful. I imagined bunk beds in the spare room, the boys playing in the backyard in matching outfits, scraped knees, and bathtime chaos. Julian and I even talked about how much our lives would change. We shared our decision with family and friends, and everyone was thrilled.

A week later, the children's social worker came over to discuss the formalities. As we sat at the kitchen table, she provided more details about the boys' background and showed us their baby books and a heartwarming video of them playing at the park. It was looking hopeful, and I was thinking, perhaps the changes I'm looking for will happen when we have the children here.

As the social worker was ending our meeting and telling us she would prepare the paperwork to move ahead, Julian got cold feet. He announced that he didn't want to move forward. The children's social worker, our social worker, and I were all stunned. My heart sank. I didn't know what to say so I didn't say anything. But deep down, I knew it was better to step back than risk the heartbreak of a failed adoption later. As he walked them out, I realized we had now found ourselves back at square one.

Fast forward in time, as we approached our fifth year in the adoption process, a new opportunity arose: two young sisters were available for adoption. In January, we spoke with the children's social worker, who agreed that we would be good parents for them. I felt a surge of happiness and relief as Julian and I were finally on the same page, genuinely ready to move forward with adopting these two lovely girls. They were cute, brown, slim girls with ponytails all over their heads, who were full of energy. After such a long journey to start our family, it felt like everything was falling into place.

Although we knew there would be challenges ahead due to their background, I was thrilled that our adoption journey would conclude with these two little girls, aged five and three. Everything was moving forward, and our assessment report was ready for submission to the adoption panel in April.

I was finishing a short-term contract that would conveniently end one month before the girls' arrival, giving me a month to prepare. However, after my contract ended in February, I couldn't reach the children's social worker—she didn't return my calls, and we started receiving updates from a third party instead. Something felt off, but Julian and I continued making plans for their arrival in April.

In early February, we learned of an upcoming court case to determine if the children would return to the council's custody so we could adopt them. The night before the court date in mid-February, we received an unexpected call from the children's advocate. The timing was odd as we hadn't spoken with the advocate in months. She asked if we would be open to allowing the girls to visit with their birth mother after we adopted them. While we had been encouraged to say we would, Julian and I stood firm and said, "Absolutely not." This time, we were in full agreement. We knew the disruptions their mother had caused while the girls were in care. Why adopt children we wanted to raise as our own only to let them see their birth mother, who could potentially unsettle their lives again? Raising children is challenging enough; raising children torn between us and their birth mother would be even harder. We knew it would only deepen their longing for her and cause heartache for all of us.

The children's advocate told us that if we refused to grant the girls access to see their mother, she would recommend to the courts that we not be given adoption rights. We replied, "Okay."

I told Julian I didn't want us to simply be babysitters—I wanted us to be their parents, and he agreed wholeheartedly. Who would want to adopt children, only to allow them visits with the very person whose actions had led to their need for care? It didn't seem like the way to provide a stable, nurturing environment for the girls to grow up in.

The next day, we anxiously waited for news but heard nothing—not even the time of the court case. Two days later, we found out through a third party that the judge had placed the sisters back with their mother. What?! We were stunned. No wonder we'd been kept in the dark; it seemed they'd already planned to reunite the girls with their mother. If she didn't want them, it felt like we were simply the backup plan.

I was overwhelmed with anger and heartbreak, watching what I thought would be the start of our family crumble into nothing. It felt like there had been things going on behind the scenes. There was nothing more to be said or done. I knew I had to let this chapter of us trying to be parents come to an end.

We remained on the adoption registry for another year, but over time, the adoption landscape changed significantly.

Fewer children were being put up for adoption, as more emphasis was placed on finding family members who could adopt. As the number of eligible children declined, we saw fewer profiles to consider. Eventually, the agency called us in to discuss whether we wanted to continue pursuing adoption. By then, we knew we had reached the end of the road. After years of trying without success, we came to terms with the decision not to pursue adoption any further. It was time to let go of that dream.

As Julian and I arrived for our final appointment, memories of our first visit flooded back. I recalled sitting in this waiting area, feeling hopeful and excited about the possibility of building a family, looking at all the pamphlets about adoption and the resources available. Back then, I thought this journey would fulfil Julian's early comment about us adopting.

We had imagined the faces of children waiting to be chosen, wondered about the backgrounds they'd come from, and felt uncertain about the process and whether we'd be approved. But, six years later, as we sat in the same waiting area, we knew our journey had reached its end. This was the final chapter for us as approved adopters and would-be parents. Despite our hopes and efforts, this path had proven unfruitful. It hadn't turned out the way we had once envisioned.

Julian had told me beforehand that he knew we were being called in to close the adoption chapter and that he would let them know we wanted to be removed from the adopter list before they had the chance to say it. When the head of the agency and our social worker joined us, the same women who were so excited to see us at the adoption information event, after the usual pleasantries, they explained that they had done all they could to find a match but, after all this time, their resources would be better directed toward other hopeful couples. We agreed, thanked them for their support, and left. I felt numb—no emotion left.

And so, after six years on this adoption journey, we found ourselves with no child and only a trail of losses. What was next for us? We continued going through the motions of marriage, but we had become more like roommates than partners.

I felt so disappointed—and truthfully, resentful—towards Julian. I longed for him to take the lead when it came to starting a family. I didn't want to be the one pushing, urging, and initiating everything. I didn't need him to have all the answers, just to be willing to enter the conversation with me; openly, honestly, as a partner.

Why didn't he want to adopt those children we had seen? Was he holding on to the freedom that came with not having kids? Or was it fear? Fear of fatherhood shaped by his own upbringing, where his father was present but never really involved, and his mother made all the decisions? Was he looking for me to make all the decisions and he would go along with it?

I couldn't get anything out of him. He shut down, and I was left feeling utterly alone. We still shared the same bed, but there was no intimacy. Our words revolved around work, weekend errands, and surface-level chatter—but never the thing that was quietly tearing us apart.

I wasn't one of those women who spent her life dreaming of motherhood, but I had hoped to break away from the legacy of my own upbringing. I wanted to give my child the love and security my birth mother hadn't given me. I imagined that our marriage, our family, and our children would redeem the wrongs of my past. But after fifteen years of marriage, that redemption hadn't come. None of the dreams I'd held close had been fulfilled.

CHAPTER 5

Yeah, Everything's Fine!

Through all these trials, I put on my usual mask, acting unfazed by everything I was going through, just as I always had. I assured my family and friends that I was fine, pretending that nothing was wrong. But in hindsight, I was facing one of the most challenging times of my life.

In every setting, I kept up appearances, wearing my 'happy face.' At work, I didn't even confide in my managers, even though I often needed time off for appointments. I realized I'd taken my unbothered approach too far when I continued contributing to baby shower gifts and signing maternity leave cards, all while harboring a quiet envy for these women. I was yearning for the day when I'd have my own baby and baby shower, just as I'd imagined it: an elegant afternoon tea with cakes, floral arrangements everywhere, and a wall of flowers. I wanted to be the center of attention, with a life growing inside me—a baby I could love and nurture. I wanted a mini-me who would love me unconditionally. Someone to share life with and shower with love and to pass on my knowledge, so they wouldn't have to struggle as I had; having a mother who didn't want them and thought their pregnancy had messed up their life. I wanted to experience the deep connection of having a mother-child bond and, above all, to finally be a mother myself.

Another time I pretended everything was fine was at my friend, Kendra's, baby shower. Kendra and Gail, my other closest friend, were pregnant at the same time. After playing games and opening the presents, someone asked them to stand belly to belly for a photo, and what did I do? You guessed it—I jumped up to take the picture . . . on my own camera. Ha! It's amazing, really, how childless women manage to keep it together as much as we do!

As I took those photos, I couldn't help but wish it was all three of us going through pregnancy together—three baby bumps instead of two. I wondered why it wasn't my turn to join them. I longed to have my own big belly, a swollen nose, waddling around greeting everyone, unbalanced as I hugged friends and too uncomfortable to sit down myself.

Later, Gail pulled me to the side and said, "Salise, my husband had a dream all three of us were pregnant together." That comment sparked a glimmer of hope in me, and I thought, 'Maybe it will happen by the time they're having their second child.'

I asked, "Do your husband's dreams usually come true?"

She replied, "Yes, they often do."

But that dream never materialized. Their second pregnancies and births came and went, and still, I hadn't joined them in this experience.

How do we bear the torture we inflict on ourselves by striving to meet the societal and self-imposed standard of being unbothered? I couldn't imagine the shock or fallout if I were to break down, throw a tantrum, or make a scene at any of the baby showers I attended over the years—yet I wanted to. I wanted to release all that pent-up pain and frustration.

At the same time, I was genuinely happy for my friends and wanted to show them love, celebrate with them, and buy adorable little outfits for their babies. But beneath the surface, I felt the sting of my own longing. I was torn between joy for them and sadness for myself, and that inner conflict left me feeling guilty and disappointed in my own mixed emotions.

A year after my fertility treatment, Tosin, a church friend, reached out and suggested we meet up. We met at Angel tube station and walked around until we found a quiet little bar which was dimly lit with red lighting. Nervously, she said, "God wants me to tell you something," and opened her Bible.

I had no idea what to expect as she began reading several verses, but as I listened, I realized she was sharing a prophecy: God wanted me to know that His desire was for me to have a child.

She read several Bible verses to me, and I've since turned them into personal affirmations and confessions.

Here's how they guide me now:

*I rejoice and am highly favored. The Lord is with me.
Blessed am I before all other women. I am not afraid, for I
have found favor with God. I have conceived in my womb
and will give birth to [a child.] For with God, nothing is
impossible. Luke 1:28-31*

*I am blessed above all people; there is not a male or female
barren among me. My husband and I are not barren. We
are fruitful in the name of Jesus. Deuteronomy 7:14*

*The Lord has taken away from my husband and me all
sickness and disease. I shall not suffer miscarriage nor be
barren. God will fulfil the number of my days of pregnancy
and life. Exodus 23:25-26*

God is not a respecter of persons. Acts 10:34

*Like God did when Boaz took Ruth, and she became his
wife. He went in to her and the Lord gave her conception
and she bore a son. The Lord has caused me to conceive.
Ruth 4:13*

*With Hannah, the Lord remembered her. And it came to
pass in the process of time that Hannah conceived and
bore a son and named him Samuel, which means because
I have asked for him from the Lord. Like Hannah, I have
conceived and will deliver [a son] in Jesus' name.
1 Samuel 1:19, 20*

For with God, nothing is impossible. Luke 1:37

I was stunned. God wanted me to have a child? I thanked Tosin for sharing this message, and I thanked God as well. After receiving this prophecy, I knew I needed to build my faith to bring this promise to life. God was ready for me to have this baby, and so was I.

I committed myself to strengthening my faith in these words. I turned the Bible verses into affirmations, reading and repeating them daily. I found books and CDs with promises of conception from the stories of women in the Bible who had experienced similar journeys. I even created a vision board of God's promises and hung it inside my bathroom cabinet, where I could see it each day and speak those affirmations aloud.

With God's promise that He wanted me to have a child still unfulfilled, I began to question: 'Why was having a child so important to me?' Although it took me years to look deeply into my heart, I eventually understood that my desire stemmed from a longing to heal and complete the experience I missed by growing up without my birth mother.

I yearned for a relationship where someone would celebrate me, love me unconditionally, and share in those special mother-daughter moments like shopping trips or late-night talks, giving me advice and guidance for my life. While my stepmother, who has been in my life since I was a preteen, has been wonderful, our relationship didn't fill that specific void. I realized, much later, that this missing relationship dynamic—the mother-daughter bond I had longed for—was the deepest, darkest reason why I wanted, and felt I needed, to have children.

In my early fifties, after seventeen years of marriage, I realized I was still longing for a restored relationship with my birth mother. But I had to face the reality: "Salise, your mother is over eighty. The dreams you have of a happy, healed relationship are unlikely to come true." Although I held onto faith that God might bring restoration, it didn't seem likely. I noticed some changes in her—she'd grown kinder, trying to ask how I was doing—but I struggled to trust her. Her past hurts had left me wary, convinced she could turn on me at any moment.

Over the last twenty years, my birth mother and I would sometimes go a year or more without speaking, which was painful because there was so much I wanted to share with her. She had taken me to London and around Europe as a high school graduation present. And now that I was living here, I had seen and explored so much more of what we experienced together.

Yet, when we did talk, the conversation always centered around her. She'd tell me random details, like her late-night calls into the radio talk show, her claim to be the reincarnation of Cleopatra, or the history of Africa once being called Nigritia, working for top executives at the banks in Los Angeles, or competing in tennis tournaments. Her stories were intriguing, but over the years, I heard them so many times that they became part of our hour-long ritual, where I would listen to her tell me all kinds of things and then interrupt her to tell her why I was calling. I would usually say what I had to say in a very succinct manner to get it out and we would talk about it for a bit. Then the conversation would go back into her advising me about how it could have been done differently or better.

One of her favorite poems she frequently told me about her love life, as she never remarried:

I've been loved by men who were wealthy.
I've been loved by men who were poor.
I've been loved by men who had nothing and wanted no
*   more but to score.*

Our relationship was frustratingly one-sided, always on her terms. She considered herself teaching me about femininity and etiquette yet answered the phone with, "Why are you calling me?"

Despite this, I kept reaching out to her, convincing myself it was worth enduring her difficult behavior just to know her better.

I pursued a relationship with my birth mother even after everyone else had cut ties because I wanted to see if our life experiences held any similarities. I understood that her unkindness towards me and my eldest brother, Malik, stemmed from her unresolved pain over her divorce from our father, which happened when I was only a year old. She was devastated and ashamed when her seemingly perfect life fell apart. The details aren't mine to share, but I could see that wound still shaped her even now.

Subconsciously, it affected me too, especially when I discovered that my conception hadn't been something my mother desired. Recently, I uncovered how these deep-rooted feelings of rejection led me to adopt a coping mechanism of appearing unbothered whenever anything emotional happened. While I can't say these wounds have completely healed, I now recognize how they fueled my longing to have a child of my own—to rewrite my childhood story and experience a mother-child bond that I had missed growing up. I wanted to finally feel the love and connection I'd always yearned for.

I wanted to make sure that my child wouldn't have to endure the hurts and losses I faced. I wanted to break the generational cycle of pain, to end the curse, but I'm still carrying the weight of these unhealed wounds. Even now, I'm disappointed by the things that never came to be, the desire for a normal life with my birth mother.

CHAPTER 6

Unfulfilled Acts of Faith

Behind the scenes of our inability to conceive naturally, the unsuccessful fertility treatment, and the failed adoption, I still held on to that promise from God that I would have a child. But my faith began to falter. My belief was a constant rollercoaster. Some days, I would be filled with faith, hope, and certainty. Then, as soon as my period started or we missed the timing, disappointment would crash over me again.

It was emotionally exhausting. It felt more difficult going through it because I didn't know anyone who could relate to what I was experiencing. All my family and friends had children and had no trouble conceiving, leaving me to carry this struggle alone.

Even though my best friend and I prayed together weekly—and she knew about the prophecy—it wasn't until years later that I figured I needed additional support. I added my desire for conception to our prayer list and prayed with intention for it to come true. But this only led to more cycles of hope followed by disappointment. Weeks turned into months, and months stretched into years, until finally, I stopped praying for a child altogether.

I couldn't keep forcing myself to believe.

I had done everything I knew to get hold of God's promises, but disappointment continued to follow me. I'd already taken so many steps to strengthen my faith and show my belief in this promise.

Here are some of the acts of faith I carried out:

- I declared fertility affirmations almost daily, affirming God's desire for me to have a child.
- I listened to audiobooks filled with Bible verses about God answering prayers for children.
- I created vision boards with pictures of Julian and me, and babies playing in a pile of autumn leaves with matching outfits, which I hung in my bathroom so I could see them daily, visualizing the family I longed for.

One Thanksgiving, while visiting family, my mum and two aunts agreed that it had been too long of me being married and not having any children. So, they formed a circle around me and prayed for me. It was their heart's desire for me as much as it was mine.

I would often pray for my future child while wrapped in the beautiful green and burgundy prayer shawl my aunt had lovingly hand-knitted for me.

I used to love frogs, seeing them as a symbol of my journey toward love and family, like 'kissing frogs' before finding the right one to marry. When I lived in Chicago, I bought a bright, multi-colored ceramic frog bank, which I brought to London and kept for over ten years, hoping one day to pass it on to my baby.

I bought many things in faith: a pack of adorable Union Jack pacifiers, a soft plush elephant, and kept a few stuffed animals from my own childhood, all waiting for that special day. I collected classic Disney DVD movies, and children's books, including the one my mum wrote about my brother, Matthew, getting a dog. I tried not to go overboard, only buying a few baby clothes, remembering the advice to new mothers not to buy too much, as babies grow so fast. But I couldn't resist getting several adorable sets of blue onesies, dreaming of the sons I hoped to have.

We had a spare bedroom that sat empty, so I painted it a lovely shade of blue and we began calling it 'the baby's room.' I kept these baby items neatly arranged on a dresser there, ready and waiting for the day we'd welcome a little one.

Along with these acts of faith, I often heard men of God declare, "I hear the Lord saying, 'He's going to open your womb'."

Or "This time next year, you shall have a child."

Other times, they proclaimed, "This is the year of new beginnings. You are first in line. This is the year of restoration." "You will experience a double portion of God's favor. For God has appointed another seed for you instead of Abel, whom Cain killed."

Well, God was definitely speaking, but I don't know who He was talking to because there was no conception happening over here.

One Sunday, after church, a female church-goer around my age who was respected in the community, asked me out of the blue, "Are you pregnant?"

Surprised, I replied, "Not that I know of."

She seemed shocked and walked away.

I later found out that she said she had never been wrong when asking if a woman was pregnant. Apparently, it caused her to leave the church.

This wasn't the only time. Other people in church would ask if I was pregnant, too. I couldn't understand it; Julian and I weren't even intimate at the time. What were they seeing or sensing that I wasn't aware of? It left me feeling bewildered. I assumed they must have had some insight into the spiritual realm, but I wasn't knowledgeable enough about it to give it any serious thought.

Members of my church would often say things like, *"You will have a child. God will open your womb. God's going to give you double."*

Then, for three consecutive years, from August to October, my pastor would declare from the pulpit that someone's womb was open and they would have a child by this time next year, referring to Genesis 18:10 which says, *"Then the Lord said, 'I will surely return to you about this time next year, and Sarah your wife shall have a son'."*

Other couples from church would come back to testify that it had happened for them, but it was never me.

Once, I ordered a minicab and the driver, who happened to be a pastor, told me I would have a child within the year.

One evening, I felt an urge to go home and initiate intimacy, hoping it might rekindle our connection and open a door to conception. But when my efforts fell flat, I eventually went to sleep.

The next morning, I questioned that feeling and asked Julian if he'd also felt like we should have been intimate. To my surprise, he said he did have the same inclination but hadn't put in any effort either. Another missed opportunity.

It struck me how heartbreaking this must be for couples trying to conceive—the knowledge that there are fleeting moments when intimacy might be meant to happen, but they pass by because we don't take action. It's a painful reminder of how easily potential chances can slip away.

I remember a time when everything seemed perfectly aligned for us to conceive. We were intimate on the exact day I noticed my egg white-looking cervical mucus.

The next morning, as I looked at myself in the bathroom mirror, I thought excitedly, 'I wonder if I'm pregnant.' But then I heard an inner voice sharply say, 'No!'

I was taken aback, wondering what that could mean, but I brushed it off, not wanting to believe it was anything other than a passing thought. Yet, I couldn't shake the feeling, and I resigned myself to the likelihood that conception hadn't happened and that my period would come in a couple of weeks. I was heartbroken. How was I supposed to keep living with this kind of repeated disappointment and sense of defeat?

Another missed opportunity came when my godson, in his innocent honesty, asked me why I didn't have any children. I didn't have a real answer for him, so I simply said, "Sometimes things just don't happen like we plan."

Without missing a beat, he told me, "Go home and have sex with your husband." So direct and truthful. I couldn't help but smile at his simplicity, but inside I thought, 'It's not that easy. We haven't been intimate in a long time.'

That was about a year after our adoption plans had fallen through, and Julian and I had been emotionally and physically disconnected for years by then. I didn't go through with it. I couldn't bear the thought of another disappointment or rejection. But looking back, I wonder if maybe, just maybe, that could have been the moment for us to conceive.

Imagine all the children I've watched grow up in church over fifteen years, all the baby dedications I've sat through. I've seen couples marry, get pregnant, and stand before the congregation to dedicate their children to God—some dedicating multiple babies over the years. I pictured myself up there one day, dedicating my own child, but year after year passed without God's promise manifesting.

How do you live with an unfulfilled promise from God? I knew God doesn't lie, so I assumed the problem had to be me. After all these years, my faith had faded; I barely believed it anymore. I felt like I'd missed it. I missed God's timing. I missed my season. I hadn't done what I was supposed to do. I hadn't listened properly. I hadn't been obedient enough. Maybe I hadn't sown enough, prayed enough, or believed enough. I thought I hadn't confessed His promises with enough conviction or meditated on them enough. Maybe I just didn't deserve it. Perhaps God was angry at me, wanting to teach me something that I'd failed to learn.

By this point, my emotions had been shut down for so long that none of it seemed to matter anymore. I wasn't bothered by it. Seeing babies in prams didn't make me feel happy or broody. Pregnant women walking by didn't stir any anger or jealousy. I wasn't fazed by baby shower invitations or birth announcements. I had simply grown used to time passing while my friends' children grew older and reached new milestones.

On top of all these disappointments, I was just tired of trying, of hoping, and of managing the emotional toll that came with trying to make a baby. I told myself, "Salise, you can't keep crying about this every month."

One day, I walked into the baby's room and looked around at all the baby items I had collected over the years: the cute outfits, the plush toys, the Union Jack pacifiers, and that beautiful, snuggly prayer shawl my aunt had lovingly made for me. One by one, I gathered them all up, packed them into a box, and tucked it away in the closet. It was time to let go of the dream I had clung to for so long. My desire wasn't as intense anymore. I had no more tears left to cry. I had tried everything I knew how to do. Over time, even the shame began to fade. People eventually stopped asking us about having children, and I just kept moving forward with life.

By the time I turned 45, the maximum age for receiving fertility treatments in the UK, the pressure was finally off. There was nothing more to strive for, no looming deadlines, and no more expectations to meet. It was a strange kind of relief.

Even though there were no longer medical avenues available to me, the desire for a child and a family still lingered in my heart. I was reminded of this about five years after we were removed from the adoption registry, during a conversation with a girlfriend. I mentioned wanting a child, and Adrianna responded, "Oh, you must be past the age of wanting children by now." Her comment surprised me. Just because I'm older doesn't mean I've settled in my heart or life not to have children. The ticking of a biological clock doesn't erase a desire. If I could have a child at my age, I would. I still think about the treehouse my daddy said he would build for me but never did and I still wish I had it. Desires don't vanish because of an arbitrary timeline. That said, I also acknowledge that God's promise to me has not yet come to pass, and I would love for it to.

The scriptures remind me that God's word does not return void. I often think about Sarai, later known as Sarah, who bore a son in her old age. Initially, she laughed at the idea of conceiving when it seemed impossible, but years later, she gave birth to Isaac, even after her childbearing years had passed. I would laugh, too, if I were told now that I could conceive but with God, all things are possible.

CHAPTER 7

Too Long is Long Enough

On top of all the failures in my life, the final one was my marriage. After fifteen years, Julian and I were no longer close. We didn't talk, share our feelings, or express our disappointments, hurts, or pains. Instead of bringing us together, all our losses had driven us apart. Without communication or intimacy, our relationship became profoundly lonely. I realized I had been accepting crumbs in our marriage and had been doing so all along.

I married Julian hoping to create a relationship where we would build a life together, but that vision never materialized. I wanted us to have connections which would solidify us, like buying a home, starting a family, building financial stability, starting a business or project, or exploring the world together.

After years of our union not unfolding as I had hoped, I reflected and questioned whether staying in the marriage was still the right path for me. I thought to myself, I'm a fool for staying in this marriage. I felt foolish, looked foolish, and continually accepted foolishness.

I used to tell people a light-hearted story about when Julian and I first met, he took me to the Royal Opera House to see *Carmen* on our first date—but we never went to another opera again. I thought it was a cute 'couple's joke' and told it for years. But when I shared that story with some of Julian's friends I hadn't met before, their blank stares said everything. Their silence made me realize that the joke wasn't on him—it was on me.

Over the last five years of our eighteen-year marriage, as our relationship seemed to deteriorate more rapidly, I started noticing the clues and red flags that had been there all along. I began asking myself, 'Why am I still in this relationship?'

Julian's health was worsening as he continued drinking with his friends twice a week, often footing the bill for everyone. On top of that, he spent heavily on gambling, plunging us into massive debt. To climb out of it, we sold our house. Our BMW and Jeep, both neglected and unmaintained, became more trouble than they were worth, so we sold them too. We downsized to a two-bedroom apartment, but things only felt bleaker.

I was nearing fifty, and we had no children, no home, no joint assets. We had nothing of real value in our apartment after we sold our home. We had not successfully navigated our challenges together. We were simply existing, living day to day as roommates, sleeping in separate bedrooms, and barely getting by, living paycheck to paycheck. It felt like there was nothing left to hold us together.

Julian seemed to avoid any responsibility, leaving me to carry the weight of our situation. More and more, it felt like I was the final thing he was trying to get rid of. I had been feeling like a burden to Julian for a long time, and one day, I finally told him. He didn't respond. He didn't deny it or reassure me otherwise—it was as if he was satisfied that I felt that way, as though now his job was done. That moment was another reality check, but I accepted it. At least we weren't having roaring fights or dealing with physical abuse. We had food to eat and a roof over our heads, and we were cordial to each other, but that was it.

Julian found more joy in spending time with his friends than with me, and I resented it. I resented the fact that, as the 'good Christian wife,' my life had deteriorated to a shadow of what it once was. We were living with so much less than I had before we got married or even earlier in our marriage. Something had shifted, but I couldn't pinpoint when or how it happened. It wasn't as though one day everything was wonderful, and the next it all fell apart. It had been a gradual, quiet decline.

My prayers didn't seem to be working. I stopped praying for a better marriage, for children, or for restoration altogether. We had gone from a beautiful life with a big house in central London, multiple cars, trips abroad, and lavish dinners, to having almost nothing. It was disheartening, but I didn't have the energy to fight for what was lost anymore. So, it stayed status quo.

As I approached my fiftieth birthday, I had a sobering realization: I couldn't keep living like this. This wasn't a marriage—it was merely an arrangement. I didn't want to be divorced, but I also couldn't imagine spending the rest of my life in this stagnant, unfulfilling situation. Things weren't improving; in fact, they were only getting worse.

We were living like college students, in a small apartment with rented furniture. 'How did this happen?' I wondered. At this stage of our lives, we should have been building stability and enjoying the fruits of our efforts, but instead, life felt like it was unravelling.

I knew I had to find a way out of this situation. Although I hadn't consciously thought about ending the marriage, it was becoming clear that I had no reason to stay. It wasn't about anger or sudden decisions—it was the quiet understanding that this life wasn't what I wanted or deserved.

Every time my brother, Luke, called, he'd ask me, "When are you going to leave him?"

I never had an answer. I wasn't ready. I had three brothers who had always looked out for me. They were protective and caring, and they wanted better for me, and I knew it. While I hadn't shared all the details of my marriage struggles over the years, it must have been obvious to them that things weren't right.

It became especially clear when my youngest brother, Miles, and his girlfriend, Madison, came to visit one Christmas. That Christmas was one of my favorites—having my family around for the holidays felt so special. How I felt about the cracks in our marriage became very evident during their visit. Julian didn't want to join us for any of the tourist activities. Miles and Madison were excited to visit our well-loved chicken doner shop on Old Kent Road, where Julian and I used to own a home, and to see the Christmas lights around Wembley. I would have loved for Julian to join us, to share in those moments, and perhaps rekindle something in our relationship but he showed no interest.

Their visit, though memorable and joyful in many ways, didn't bring us closer as a couple. Instead, it highlighted how distant we had become. Julian's disengagement was yet another reminder of how disconnected we were, even in the presence of the family who loved and supported me.

The thought that God hates divorce was a mental block I couldn't seem to overcome. It kept me tethered to the idea that I had to make things work with Julian. I tried to reconnect with him in small ways. After dinner, when we were both sitting down and relaxing, I would attempt to raise issues, hoping to open the door to meaningful conversations. But every time, he would deflect or shut it down. It felt like he was burying his head in the sand, avoiding anything uncomfortable. I didn't want to live like that anymore. I wanted to face our issues head-on.

I had hoped that having a real heart-to-heart about all the unspoken issues between us could clear the air and perhaps bring us closer. I tried many times, but those conversations never happened. Maybe he thought I was going to tell him I wanted to leave, or perhaps he couldn't face the disappointment and hurt I felt. But ending our relationship was never my intention, I just wanted us to be honest with each other, to figure out where we had gone wrong and how to move forward.

How did we get to this point? How had he become so disenchanted with me, his wife, that he didn't even feel comfortable sharing his heart? I couldn't understand how we had drifted so far apart.

Perhaps I was too much like my daddy—always trying to solve problems rather than emotionally connect or show empathy. I was the 'pull myself up by my bootstraps' type, focusing on fixing things instead of sitting with emotions. Maybe it was also the cultural differences—me being a direct American and Julian being a conflict-avoiding Brit. We had never successfully navigated conflict, and that inability to face issues together had driven us further apart. However, reality hit me hard when I went to North Carolina to visit my family for the Christmas holidays. I decided to extend my stay to celebrate my daddy's eightieth birthday in late January. As I started thinking about heading back home, I called Julian to ask about my return, and his response was, "You can stay."

That's when it finally hit me: This is over.

Julian and I had barely spoken during the six weeks I'd been away. What husband doesn't want his wife back with him? Was he enjoying the time apart? Perhaps he said it out of consideration, knowing my father's health wasn't great and wanting me to spend as much time as I needed. But deep down, it felt like he didn't want me to come back. And honestly, I didn't want to go back either. To what? Working from home? Sleeping in separate bedrooms? Barely talking to each other unless it was about groceries or dinner? How could we go so long without truly checking on each other? That phone call was the nail in the coffin. It confirmed what I had been trying to deny for so long: our marriage was done.

After I returned home, I tried once again to initiate a conversation, still holding on to the hope that we could get back on track. Julian was on the bed, and I joined him, lying beside him. I asked him about our relationship, trying to open the door to dialogue. Instead of addressing the core issues, he turned it around, saying I didn't speak to him nicely. Perhaps there was some truth to that—years ago. But at this point, it felt irrelevant. I was already emotionally drained, and when that conversation fizzled out after just a few sentences, I knew it was over. There would be no change, no reconciliation. I felt too dejected to believe anything I did at this point could make a difference. And yet, I still hadn't seriously considered leaving.

A couple of weeks later, Luke called, and I was asked again, "When are you leaving?"

I still hadn't really considered leaving. I still wasn't ready. I had been living this way for so long that it felt normal. The thought of wanting more for myself just seemed ... exhausting. On the surface, my life was full—I had a job, friends, exciting things happening in London, and I travelled often. The only thing missing was a partner who truly wanted the same things I did. Julian was a part of my life, not the center of it—and I told myself that was enough. But that was exactly the problem.

A few more months went by, and in April, my brother called again, this time urging me more firmly and said, "Your inaction is wasting time. You need to set a date!"

Whew! He wasn't playing around. Hesitant, I threw out a date, but without any real conviction. That date came and went with no action from me.

By June, when Luke called again, I was finally ready. It was already halfway through the year. I couldn't go another year like this. This time, I set a date with certainty. It was time to take the step I had been avoiding for so long.

The first step in my plan to leave was figuring out how to escape, so I rented a van. At that moment, it became real. I was officially planning to leave. Interestingly, I'd already begun retrieving things from storage over two years ago. Back then, it wasn't so much about leaving but about stopping the waste of money on items we hadn't used in over five years. It was something I'd been meaning to do, unaware that it was laying the groundwork for my departure.

Most of my belongings were already packed, having come straight out of storage. My boxes were stacked neatly on one side of the living room, while Julian's things were on the other side. He never said anything about it, and I carried on preparing to leave, sticking to my scheduled date. The silence felt like confirmation. I was doing what needed to be done.

Everything was going smoothly until the week before I was set to leave, when I received a call from the car rental agency. They informed me that the van I had reserved was unavailable, and all they had was a 4x4. I told the agent, "No, that's not going to work. I need a big, proper van."

He replied, "We don't know if we'll have one, but call us on Saturday morning, and we'll see what we can do."

It felt like a monkey wrench being thrown into my plans. I was worried, but I decided to walk by faith and trust that I'd get the van I needed.

On the morning of my move, I called the agency, but they still couldn't confirm availability. They told me to come in, so I did, arriving in the morning. My plan had been to have the van packed and be on the road by noon. When I arrived, they asked me to wait while they tried to sort things out. Time dragged painfully slowly as I tried to stay calm.

Finally, an agent came over and said they only had a four-wheel drive vehicle available and asked me to look. I knew it wasn't going to work, but I felt obliged and looked anyway. Peering into the trunk and seeing it could only hold about two suitcases, I told her, "I'm moving. This isn't going to work."

Then, I remembered seeing several vans parked along the side of the lot. I asked her to inquire about those, and she replied, "I'll see what I can do."

I started praying, "God, please let me get the van."

I called my brother, Luke who had been urging me to leave, and asked him to pray for me as well. He said he would.

Ten minutes later, the agent returned and said I could have a van but only for the weekend. I told her, "No, I need it for two weeks."

She left again and, after another nerve-wracking wait, returned with clearance for me to keep the van for two weeks. Glory to God! My door of escape had opened.

But there was still another obstacle. As I drove home, I prayed, "Lord, I need a parking space right in front of the apartment building. If this is your will, please make that happen."

When I turned onto our street, there it was, a parking space directly in front of the building, large enough for the van with room to load. I was stunned. It felt like further confirmation that I was doing the right thing.

My third prayer was for the physical strength to move my belongings. I hadn't asked friends to help; I wanted to avoid turning it into a big, dramatic event.

I prayed, "Lord, help me move all these boxes into the van, and please don't let it be too heavy or cause me pain."

God answered that prayer too. I carried about twenty boxes from the apartment, down to the lobby, and out to the van. When I was done, I wasn't aching or in pain, not even in the days that followed. God had made a way every step of the journey.

I hadn't prepared beforehand what I was going to say to Julian, but when the moment came, I told him I was leaving. His response was simple: "I knew you were." Then he called his sister on his mobile and said, "I told you she was leaving." And that was it. No discussion, no tears, no pleas for reconciliation—just a quiet acknowledgment of what we both knew had been coming. So, I walked out of the room and started getting my things ready to put into the van.

That was the most heartbreaking part. It made me realize I should have left a long time ago, as there was no fight for us, no attempt to save what we had built. I started packing up the van, making lonely trips back and forth between the apartment and the van.

As I loaded the final boxes, Julian came out with me carrying a couple of boxes. It started lightly raining as we finished. We hugged, exchanged our goodbyes, and I closed the doors to the van. As I drove away, I couldn't help but wonder, 'Is this the last time I'll ever see him?'

As I drove the large, manual van up the motorway in the rain, fear gripped me. I prayed, telling God how scared I felt. My next instinct was to declare His Word: that God is with me, that I am not afraid, and other scriptures I had held onto over the years. I spoke these words through blurred vision of tears falling as the rain streaked across the windshield. As I continued driving, the weather began to clear, and with it, my fear began to subside.

I arrived in Birmingham, my chosen destination, for a fresh start. I hadn't made any long-term housing arrangements— just a short-term rental to figure things out. Birmingham seemed smaller and more welcoming than London but relocating was far more challenging than I had anticipated.

Despite my experience moving from North Carolina to Chicago, and from Chicago to London, this was different. I had no permanent housing, no car, only the rental van. Unlike London, public transport wasn't as accessible, and a car was essential. Housing was expensive, and I found myself competing with university students for accommodation.

I was working but barely scraping by, living in temporary accommodations and moving every few weeks. After three months of this instability, my dear friend Teena drove all the way to Birmingham to see me. She came with a clear message, "You need to come back to London. No one can look after you here."

Her words struck me. I thought about it and realized she was right. I was completely alone. I could swallow my pride and admit it was time to return.

After spending a fun weekend together where I could forget all my worries, she returned home. I called my precious friend, Miranda, and shared what Teena had said. Miranda agreed and offered me to stay with her until I could get back on my feet. It was such a relief, especially since my current accommodation was ending in just a few days.

That weekend, I packed up my biggest suitcase, put the rest of my belongings in storage, and moved in with Miranda. By God's grace, within two weeks of staying with her, I found a charming little apartment. It felt like confirmation that I had made the right decision to return to London.

When I was settled into my place, I filed for divorce, and within four months, it was finalized. By the end of the year, I closed the chapter of my marriage and began a new one as an unmarried woman, ready to rebuild my life.

As easy as it seemed to begin with to start over, looking back on my life was deeply insightful. I realized just how wrong my perceptions of how life was supposed to work had been. I thought I had done everything right, only to discover that so much of it had been misguided.

I got married believing it was the right thing to do; as a Christian woman striving to meet parental, societal, and religious expectations. I thought marrying someone who I believed would be a good husband and who had my parents' approval was the right choice. I thought living according to everyone else's standards was the right path, and for a time, it seemed like everyone was pleased.

In hindsight, there were clear signs that this marriage wasn't God's plan for me—it was my plan. God had given me warnings along the way, but I had been blind to them. I was too focused on doing what I thought was right, on ticking the boxes of what a 'good Christian woman' was supposed to do and ensuring the criteria on my 'husband checklist' was matched. It was a sobering revelation to see how far I had strayed from seeking His guidance and instead leaned on my own understanding.

CHAPTER 8

Hindsight of the Unseen

Julian and I had been dating for over a year and he came home with me for the Thanksgiving holidays. After celebrating the holidays, he suggested we go engagement ring shopping at the mall. I was delighted at the thought, and agreed, as there were always large, quality diamonds in the United States. As we browsed in a jewelry store, he pointed out an emerald-cut diamond, trying to convince me it was a lovely style. It didn't appeal to me, and I continued to browse. Then I saw it—a solitaire ring that sparkled so brightly it seemed to call out to me, 'Here I am, girl, right here!' I was instantly excited. That's exactly how you should feel when you find your engagement ring. It was perfect, and Julian was so excited I loved it, that he purchased it for me.

We didn't have time to get it resized before flying back home, but the jeweler had a branch where I lived in Chicago. The salesman prepared all the necessary documentation for me to take it there and have it resized. A few days after I returned, I went to the Chicago store, filled out the paperwork, and they sent the ring off to be resized. When I came back to pick it up, my heart sank. This wasn't my engagement ring. While the band was the same, the diamond was completely different. It didn't sparkle at all. It was a dark yellow color with visible inclusions. My original diamond had been nearly flawless and almost colorless. Horrified, I immediately complained, insisting it wasn't my ring. But the staff didn't take my concerns seriously—they told me to call the police. I had never dealt with the police before, and honestly, I was scared and alone. Instead, I decided to write a letter to the company's CEO, detailing the situation and the theft. Thankfully, someone from the company reached out and scheduled a meeting. Julian flew into town to support me for this meeting.

When we met with their representatives, they presented about ten different rings as replacements. None of them matched the quality of my original diamond. I was devastated. To make matters worse, my original diamond wasn't GIA certified, so proving its value was more difficult. Reluctantly, I chose one from the options they provided. It didn't give me the same joy or excitement as my original ring, and it felt like a disappointing end to what should have been a special moment in our journey. That was the first sign that this relationship may not have been destined to work out.

Two years before I even had a boyfriend, I had found my dream wedding dress online: a stunning platinum-colored, princess-style gown. It was perfect, and I imagined myself walking down the aisle in it someday. When Julian proposed during the Christmas season, my parents already knew about the dress and decided to order it online as their wedding gift to me. The dress was being custom-made in China and was expected to arrive a few months later.

By April, however, we realized we hadn't heard anything about the order. With the wedding scheduled for July, panic set in. My parents contacted the online auction company and the seller repeatedly, but they received no response. Eventually, they had to involve the police to investigate. After months of follow-up, the Chinese police informed my parents via email that the dress was never made due to a death in the designer's family.

Time was running out, so my parents scrambled to order the dress again but from a different designer. Fortunately, the dress arrived just in time – only days before the wedding, on the Wednesday before our Saturday ceremony. It fit perfectly, but the quality was disappointing. The material was of much lower quality than expected, and the intricate detailing I loved in the original design was missing. The dress didn't look like the image I had fallen in love with.

I was heartbroken. Mum had thoughtfully purchased two backup dresses just in case the replacement didn't arrive in time. On my wedding day, I chose to wear the replacement dress because it best reflected the vision I had for my wedding, even if it wasn't the dress of my dreams. In the end, what mattered most to me was that Julian was there, waiting for me at the end of the aisle. This seemed to be another sign.

On the day of our wedding, Julian decided to take a quick nap before our evening ceremony. While the bridal party and my brothers were arriving at the venue, Julian was nowhere to be found. My brothers started looking for him, repeatedly calling his mobile phone, but he wasn't answering. It turns out he hadn't heard the calls because he was fast asleep. When he finally woke up in a panic, he saw the missed calls and quickly let my brothers know he was ready for them to pick him up. Thankfully, he made it to the venue with enough time before the ceremony started—but it was definitely a close call!

Even though my parents like Julian, there were some red flags that I ignored and wished I had taken more seriously such as his drinking and smoking habits. These were at odds with the values I grew up with. My parents rarely drank, and smoking was completely absent in our household. His lifestyle was a stark contrast to what I had known, and it unsettled me even before we married. What made it worse was his spending on these social pastimes continually grew over time.

Julian had an easy life, often achieving what he wanted without much effort or hard work. He openly admitted he didn't believe in working hard. Instead, he relied on a solid network of friends and contacts to support him whenever he needed help. While I admired his resourcefulness at first, I later realized it reflected a deeper issue of avoiding responsibility and effort.

But the biggest red flag was our lack of communication. There were key areas we never fully explored: our expectations around financial stability, holiday travel, career goals, and faith practices. While we touched on these topics, we never went deep enough to reach a shared understanding or alignment.

Julian enjoyed spending freely. At first, I found that care-free attitude attractive—until a situation came up that exposed the downside—where there was no financial cushion, no plan.

I grew up taking yearly family holidays, so travel was part of my rhythm of rest and connection. But Julian, having spent years as a consultant constantly on the move, told me he had no desire to travel more.

Looking back, the signs were there. But I turned a blind eye, convinced that love and time would smooth everything out. I didn't even realize there were blind spots until others started asking questions about our plans after we were married and I had no answers to give.

After my divorce, I had a profound moment of clarity: by not consulting God before marrying Julian, I had unknowingly set us on a path that echoed a generational pattern within my family. There were signs this marriage wasn't right for me, but whether I missed them—or simply chose to ignore them—I couldn't deny that they were there. Most importantly, I never truly sought God's guidance before saying 'I do.'

During our dating phase, I even broke up with Julian at one point. Why? His behavior didn't sit right with me. He smoked and drank more than anyone I knew. While I understood it was part of British culture, it wasn't a lifestyle I was comfortable with.

Another caution I threw to the wind was his spending habits. Julian was a big spender and seemed very generous, which I initially found charming. But in hindsight, his approach to money wasn't secure or sustainable. What once seemed like generosity revealed itself as a lack of financial discipline, which later became a significant factor in our struggles.

When we got back together and started talking about marriage, I had a moment where I considered asking God if Julian was the one for me. But I dismissed the thought almost immediately. Deep down, I think I knew God's answer would have been a firm no. I didn't want to hear that, so I avoided asking. I was determined to make my own decision, convinced that because I felt we could have a happy life together and my parents liked him, I was doing the right thing.

I overrode every caution, every doubt, and every thought that urged me not to proceed. And in the end, our marriage failed. Ignoring God's desire to lead me placed me into a situation that might have been avoided if I had chosen humility over self-reliance and resisted the urge to trust my own judgement.

CHAPTER 9

The Idols We Carry Are Heavy

Being married to a British man, living abroad, and owning a large home in Central London were idols. Longing for a baby so they wouldn't have to endure the childhood woes I once faced, and hoping to rewrite my story through them, had become idols in my heart.

These desires weren't idols because they were inherently wrong; they became idols because I believed they would give me attention and validate my life. I believed that by doing the 'right' thing, I would receive the unmet needs for love and unconditional acceptance I longed for.

I was seeking a form of idol status as well—wanting others to look at me and see what I had, what I had done, what I had accomplished—to give me attention and adoration. I thought I could rectify my past, break the curse of my parents' divorce, and avoid being single in my later years. I was mistaken.

I came to understand that I was wrong to think I knew best what was good for me. I had placed my hopes and happiness on these external things, expecting them to complete me, but they couldn't.

Being married and having a child was all about me. Look what I've got. Look what I've done. Look at what I've accomplished. I've rectified my past. I've broken the curse of divorce that my parents had. I've broken the curse by being able to give my child everything I didn't have. I've broken the curse of not being single in my later years. What I wanted, what I thought I deserved; no person, title, or achievement could ever be enough to fill that void.

This was a hard realization to confront, and it came to me in the most unexpected way. It was when Julian bought me flowers two years before we separated. He was heading out to the grocery store with a list I'd given him, and just as he was walking out the door, I added, 'A bouquet of flowers' to the list. When he came back, he surprised me with a tall, vibrant purple orchid. Given the state of our dissolving marriage, it was more than I expected. I was so happy and thanked him sincerely. The first thing I wanted to do was share this moment on Facebook. I took a selfie with the beautiful orchid, wrote a grateful post tagging Julian, and hit 'Post.' But as soon as I did, I was overwhelmed by a sudden, crushing emptiness. That orchid—and every flower in the world—couldn't fill the gaping hole of emptiness in my soul at that moment. It was shocking, like staring into an abyss. I mentally saw that orchid falling into a vast, dark pit, and listened. It never seemed to reach the bottom. The emptiness was endless, like a bottomless void. I realized then that no number of flowers, no grand gestures, and no social media validation could ever fill that deep darkness inside me.

I sat with the heavy question: 'How had I become so empty?' It was a moment of painful clarity—one that forced me to acknowledge how much I had been trying to fill my soul with external things that could never truly satisfy me.

I believed that fulfilling societal and Christian norms would bring me acceptance, create the life I wanted and deserved, and ultimately show me unconditional love. But I've learned the hard truth: my ways are not higher than God's ways.

The decisions I made for how I thought my life should unfold weren't the best ones for me. I was chasing what seemed glamorous, fulfilling, and right in the eyes of the world, but they left me empty. Only through the wisdom of time and painful experiences did I come to realize that I had forsaken my relationship with God in pursuit of these fleeting, unfulfilling pursuits. What I thought would bring me joy and purpose only highlighted how far I had strayed from His guidance.

After divorcing Julian, I was faced with the sobering reality of the losses behind me. The weight of all I had endured was undeniable. As hard as those experiences were, I knew I had to pick myself up and move forward. Honestly, I can't fully explain how I made it through without losing my mind.

I've now come to understand that those difficult times were just seasons—a natural part of the rhythm of life. They weren't failures because Julian was a terrible person; they happened because I chose to do what I wanted to do. Sometimes, that's simply how life unfolds.

I had to confront a hard truth about myself: I wanted to be appreciated and seen as valuable. I craved validation in a way that was ultimately desiring to be worshipped. And seeking that kind of attention or fulfilment will always lead to the wrong decisions. It was a painful but necessary lesson in letting go of false idols and realigning my priorities with God's will.

How can two walk together unless they have agreed? Julian and I were never on the same page—whether it was about morals, values, goals, what we wanted for our life and family, how to handle money, or most importantly, our relationship with God. These differences didn't seem to matter much in the beginning, but over time, our lack of agreement became a significant barrier. We couldn't move forward because we weren't aligned. Instead, we stayed stagnant, and eventually, things started to decline. If you're not moving forward, you're regressing.

For the first ten years of our marriage, everything seemed to be going well. We owned a large four-bedroom home, two luxury cars, and had good salaries. But somewhere along the way, things changed. I looked up one day and saw that Julian had maxed out our credit cards, we were living off our overdraft, and bills were piling up, unpaid. Our debts were so overwhelming that we couldn't keep up and were forced to sell the house. Even after selling it, our expenses still exceeded our income. The money we had left from the house sale dwindled rapidly.

I was scared, embarrassed, and ashamed. I couldn't live like that anymore. I hadn't grown up in an environment of scarcity, and the thought of becoming homeless terrified me. I found myself living at a level no better than when I had just graduated from college. Our lives weren't improving with time, which seemed to contradict God's promises of blessings and abundance. I struggled to reconcile this reality with the years I'd spent praying for Julian, for our marriage, and serving faithfully in church.

Eventually, I realized the core issue: Julian didn't have the capacity to worship me anymore. He had given me all that he had. And I think he knew in the beginning that he didn't have the capacity to continually provide me with all that I wanted, which is probably why we never resolved our differences of opinion. Perhaps he thought if he said things in opposition to my desires, I would walk away. And possibly that is why I felt like I was the burden he was trying to get rid of at the end of our marriage. It was too big of a burden to carry, and it shouldn't have been his anyway. Still, I knew I couldn't stay stuck. I couldn't keep living like my life was over just because it hadn't turned out the way I wanted it to. There was still so much more of life I wanted to experience. Deep down, I knew I was bigger than the life I was living, and I had to step out of the rut I had been stuck in to reclaim my purpose and joy.

CHAPTER 10

It's Not You. It's Me.

Two years before getting married, I dedicated my life to God and was baptized. A year later, I was the closest to God I'd ever been. I had just completed a twelve-week intercessory prayer course through a ministry in Chicago, which deepened my spiritual walk.

One Saturday morning, about three months before our wedding, I was praying when I had a vision. I saw a cream-colored card, about the size of a postcard, with a blue ribbon tied like a bow at the top. I instantly knew it was a birth announcement, though I couldn't make out the details. I felt led to pray for the birth of this baby and for his life and purpose. I was curious. Who could be pregnant?

After praying, I called three of my girlfriends to ask if they were expecting, but none of them were. I checked with my family, and no one was pregnant either. Even Mum, who often had symbolic dreams of fish when someone was pregnant, hadn't had any such dreams.

To this day, I don't know who God had me praying for in that moment. But I'm humbled that He chose to reveal it to me and allowed me to intercede for this unknown child. It was a powerful reminder of the way God invites us into His plans, even when we don't fully understand them.

Unfortunately, even though I was just a few months away from getting married, I still wouldn't bring myself to ask Him if Julian was the man I should marry. Deep down, I feared He would say, "No."

Growing up, I had heard "no" so many times from my parents, teachers, aunties, elders, and anyone in authority over me. I was always doing what I was told, following their guidance—even though I now realize their advice wasn't always the best for me. Obeying them kept the peace and didn't result in anyone being upset with me.

I didn't even want to consider the possibility that God might not want me to marry Julian. I couldn't face the thought that He might have a different plan for my life. I wanted the family, the dream of a big house with a white picket fence—the American dream. I was in my thirties, and I knew that for many women, proposals were rare, maybe once or twice in a lifetime. I told myself this was my chance. My parents liked Julian better than my ex, we were in love, and I believed we could get along and be happy together. But if I'm honest, I wanted to do what I wanted to do. I thought I had made a great, significant decision for myself. I thought I was right. In hindsight, though, my desire to have my way was a delusion—a trap set by the enemy.

I was also hesitant to seek God's input because all my life, I had lived complying with the expectations of my father and everyone else who had input into my decisions. Moving away from home gave me a sense of freedom I had never experienced before, and I wanted to fully embrace it. This was my chance to make my own choices, to chart my own path. But in choosing to silence God's voice, I made a decision that would have consequences far beyond what I could see at the time.

When I was engaged, I made a bold declaration to God: "Give me three years to be a wife, and I'll come back to You." My reason was simple: I wanted to focus on being a wife and building a life, a home, and a family with Julian in those early years.

Amazingly, He graciously accepted my terms. True to His nature, three years into my marriage, I felt a nudge in my spirit—a gentle but unmistakable call to return to Him. (I think that is why Jesus went to dinner at Zacchaeus, the tax collector's house. God likes that people pay what they owe.) I kept my word, sought Him again, and found a church home.

Looking back now, I see how delusional I was. Who did I think I was to believe I could take on everything—being a wife, working full-time, building a marriage, starting a family, relocating abroad, and integrating into my husband's family—all without God? It's almost laughable. I thought I could manage it on my own, but the truth is, I was utterly naive. Without God, I was trying to carry burdens I was never meant to bear alone. That realization has stayed with me as a humbling reminder of my need for Him in every season of life.

A significant part of the reason I decided to marry Julian was because my daddy encouraged me to. I've always wanted to please Daddy, and I listened when he told me, "If Julian has any conversations with you about marriage, make sure he knows you will say yes to his proposal." I knew Daddy had my best interests at heart. But in hindsight, I realize that I regarded his voice higher than God's.

This awareness has given me some deeper insight into why God commands us to honor and obey our parents—and why there is a blessing attached to keeping that commandment. It's because parents can often see more clearly when their children are heading down the same destructive paths, they themselves once walked. By listening to their wisdom, we can avoid replicating their same mistakes and breaking generational patterns of pain. But the opposite is also true: when we place their advice above God's guidance, even with the best intentions, we risk creating new cycles of disobedience and heartbreak.

From when I was baptized to my wedding day, God was an important part of my life, but I hadn't fully made Him Lord over my life. I hadn't submitted my will to His. Instead, I was serving God on my own terms, following Him in a way that aligned with my plans rather than surrendering to His. It is a humbling truth to admit, but it's also a lesson that has helped me understand the importance of true submission to God's desires for my life.

Looking back, I can see several reasons why I silenced that voice and made the decision on my own. Julian ticked nearly every box on my 'husband checklist.' I thought long and hard about the qualities that would be a great match for me and was excited that I'd met someone who reflected exactly what I wanted and what was best for me. I trusted my judgment more than I trusted God's.

I didn't want to end up like my birth mother. She had become bitter and disappointed with life, living alone and unmarried in her later years. She had chosen to live isolated from her family and children. I knew that I didn't want that path for myself and was determined to avoid that outcome at all costs.

I liked Julian as a person. I thought that liking someone in addition to loving them was enough to sustain a marriage. After all, I'd seen plenty of couples who didn't seem to even like each other after years of marriage, let alone love each other. Liking Julian felt like a solid foundation.

My parents approved of him. My family—especially my parents and siblings—absolutely abhorred my last boyfriend. That experience made me reconsider my perspective that only my feelings mattered in choosing a life partner. I decided that for the sake of my family, who I wanted to continue spending time with, I needed someone they liked too—and Julian fit the bill.

Julian said he prayed every night. For me, this was significant. It was the most I had heard any man say about having a relationship with God, and I took it as a positive sign. If he had God in his life, I was choosing a Godly man. How could this not be right?

With all these reasons, I convinced myself I was making the right decision and felt content with the path I was taking. I was so focused on what seemed logical and best aligned with my desires. I am remorseful to look back and understand how I allowed my fears, logic, and external validation to drown out God's voice.

CHAPTER 11

A Different Reconciliation

I've had a complex relationship with my birth mother after she relinquished me at five years old to be raised by my father. As an adult, I often reached out to her, eager to learn if there were patterns in our upbringing and marital relationships. I enquired about her childhood experiences, how she and Daddy met, and the challenges they faced in their relationship. What surprised me most was discovering the similarities in our lives, despite spending less than three hundred and sixty-five days together since I was five years old.

She and I had to contend with external forces that strained our marriages. We shared the experience of having husbands who seemed to enjoy being out more than they valued being at home. While my marriage lasted eighteen years—the same length as Julian's parents' marriage— my birth mother and I ultimately made the decision to leave our husbands. Even though the circumstances and durations of our relationships were different, the outcome was eerily similar. It was a disheartening discovery of how generational patterns can subtly repeat themselves even without being under the influence of a parent.

A few months ago, my pastor preached about generational curses and how, as God's children, we are no longer under the curse because Jesus died on the cross as a sacrifice for our sins. Through His sacrifice, the curses of sin no longer apply to us. I had heard these biblical truths many times before and believed them, but as I listened, I couldn't help but reflect on how my life didn't seem to reflect the abundance of blessings that Jesus died for me to have. There was a clear disconnect.

In my marriage, there was no long-term abundance of blessings—not in our peace, health, careers, or finances. Toward the end, everything deteriorated. Yet, I was doing all the things I thought a faithful Christian should do. I attended church regularly, prayed consistently, served as a church leader, took Holy Communion, and was a cheerful giver of tithes and offerings. Still, my life didn't reflect the blessings of God's promises.

As I listened to the pastor's message, I asked God: 'How do I reconcile the fact that my life doesn't reflect Your abundant blessings, even though Your Word says the curse has been paid for by Jesus' death on the cross?'

In that moment, I heard the Holy Spirit recall to me the book of Deuteronomy, Chapter 28. Hopefully, you're familiar with it. It was the chapter where God outlines blessings or curses for His children, depending on their obedience. It became clear that the root of the disconnect wasn't about curses but about obedience. While Jesus freed me from the curse of sin, the blessings I longed for required my alignment with God's will—obedience to His Word.

As I processed what I had just heard, it made sense. This awareness was a humbling and eye-opening moment, showing me how critical it is to examine not just our actions but the heart behind them. It's not about ticking religious boxes but truly living in alignment with God's desires for our lives.

These were the Bible verses that came to mind:

If you diligently obey the voice of the LORD your God, to observe carefully all His commandments which I command you today, that the Lord your God will set you high above all nations of the earth.
2 And all these blessings shall come upon you and overtake you, because you obey the voice of the LORD your God.
Deuteronomy 28:1

But it shall come to pass, if you do not obey the voice of the LORD your God, to observe carefully all His commandments and His statues which I command you today, that all these curses will come upon you and overtake you
Deuteronomy 28:15

God is not a man, that He should lie, nor a son of man, that He should repent. Has He said, and will He not do? Or has He spoken, and will He not make it good? Number 23:19

That was so deep. My disobedience to God played a significant role as to why there was no long-term fruitfulness in my marriage. Now it made sense. By not following God's commandment of obedience and not seeking His guidance when I decided to marry Julian, I had stepped outside of His plan for my life. While His grace is abundant, He calls us to walk in obedience so that His blessings can flow freely in our lives.

The disobedience wasn't just on my side, Julian was disobedient to God as well. We both had rebellious streaks in us, putting ourselves first and that left little room for God's presence to be displayed in our lives and our marriage. It opens a path for destruction to take hold.

Another form of disobedience I exhibited was seeking instant gratification and insisting on getting my way. An idol is anything that demands immediate satisfaction or threatens emotional turmoil. Its 'wrath,' if denied. If you find yourself overwhelmed with emotional angst when you don't get your way, it reveals a deeper issue: the desire to be worshiped. Is that why you want to be a mother or to be married?

Needing to be satisfied immediately elevates you to the position of an idol. Why must you get your way? Because, at its core, it reflects that you require external validation and that someone or something can provide what you need. You feel compelled to prove to yourself or the world that you are loved, accepted, respected, or worthy, no matter the cost.

This mindset demonstrates that God is not your true source of love, acceptance, provision, or protection. He is meant to be your Father, your Husband, your closest friend, your defender, and your Savior. But if you're making rash decisions without seeking His guidance, you're putting your wants and needs above His desires for you. God's desires are always for your ultimate good, even if it means waiting or taking a different path than you had planned.

When you choose your way over His, it's almost inevitable that regrets will follow. Instantaneous, flesh-driven decisions don't align with the Spirit of God, and as a result, failure or disappointment is often the outcome. The lesson here is clear: true fulfilment and peace come only when we trust God as our source and align our choices with His will, rather than chasing fleeting, self-centered desires.

Yet life has a way of teaching us resilience. Through all the losses we face, we learn that we must continue moving forward. I longed for a life that reflected all the goodness expected from following societal, religious, and cultural standards but my heart was misaligned.

CHAPTER 12

Reclaiming Hope

A couple of years after my divorce, I found myself reflecting on my life and all the losses I'd experienced. Growing up without my birth mother was an early loss that shaped me. Later, being a childless woman when I never wanted to be one became another profound loss. For a long time, I thought my divorce and barrenness were the major losses of my life. But as I looked closer, I realized loss had always been present in many forms.

There were losses in my romantic relationships and in my career, for example, when I was made redundant. There were smaller, yet painful moments of loss, like when my wedding dress never arrived or when my engagement ring diamond was stolen. I've lost handbags, phones, and even years of my life without my birth mother. Friendships ended without explanation. Opportunities slipped away; whether it was not spending more time with Daddy before he passed, not asking for that promotion or salary increase at work, or simply not taking the chances I should have.

Loss comes in countless ways. Yet, despite all these challenges, I've always found the strength to carry on. Life has shown me that resilience isn't just about bouncing back from the big losses, but also navigating the smaller, everyday ones and continuing forward with hope and determination.

Maybe it was the passing of time, or maybe it was my faith, but I've come to realize that humans were created to be resilient. There's a biblical passage, John 16:33 that says, *"In the world you will have trouble, but be of good cheer, for I have overcome the world."*

This reminds me that trouble is inevitable, but it doesn't have to break us. Life is full of mountains and valleys. The question is: Can you stand the storm long enough to get through it?

I'm reminded of when Jesus said to His disciples, "Let us go over to the other side." He was asleep in the boat as the wind and storms raged around them. Jesus knew there was somewhere He was going, a destination He was determined to reach. But the disciples, like so many of us, didn't expect to face storms on the way.

We think that if we're in a nice, sturdy boat, we will arrive at our destination well-rested and ready for what's next. That's how I thought my married life would go. I thought being married to a good man was my weatherproof boat. I thought I'd rest comfortably in our beautiful, spacious London home.

Then the storms came. Infertility was one of them, shaking everything I thought was secure. I hadn't prepared for a storm that big. I thought smooth sailing was guaranteed.

But storms test us, and they reveal where our true foundation lies.

There's another powerful Biblical passage where the prophet Elijah tells his servant to look for a cloud the size of a man's hand—a small sign that a massive storm was on the horizon. Elijah knew that when the rain started, it would come as a deluge. Life is often like that. We don't know the size or intensity of the storm headed our way, but we need to be prepared—not just to survive it but to rebuild if it disrupts our comfort zones.

The storms of life come, but resilience, faith, and trust in God's promises are what carried me through to the other side.

My life felt shattered as we aged beyond childbearing years, were removed from the adoption registry, and finalized our divorce. The weight of these losses left me wondering how I would ever rebuild after such significant heartbreak. Yet, somehow, I persevered.

During those bleak days, I leaned into self-care. I joined a singing academy and took up horse riding—two activities I never imagined myself pursuing. It took courage to step out and try something new, but it was worth it. These interests weren't things I had dreamed of doing; they were simply steps I took to remind myself that life was still moving forward, even when I felt stuck.

I realized I didn't want to remain in an unhappy marriage for another decade or more, watching life pass me by. Choosing to focus on myself, rediscovering activities which brought me joy, and seeking God more became my way of reclaiming hope and rebuilding my life one day at a time.

CHAPTER 13

The Perseverance Perspective

I always remember the day of my granddaddy's funeral. Forest was such a special man to me, even though he lived in another state, and I didn't get to see him often. His sense of humor always stood out; it was one of the things I loved most about him.

I will never forget the time he visited us in North Carolina unexpectedly. I saw him coming up the driveway, and I ran out to meet him, throwing my arms around him for a big hug. I looked around, curious, and asked, "Who did you come with?"

Without missing a beat, he replied, "J.C."

I was confused. I didn't know of any family member named J.C. and he came out of the car alone, so I asked, "Who is that?"

He grinned and said, "Jesus Christ."

That was Granddaddy Forest—always quick with a joke but leaving you with something meaningful to think about. It's little memories like these that keep him alive in my heart.

Granddaddy Forest's funeral was one of the first I attended as a teenager, and I remember feeling utterly heartbroken. As I sat in the church, my birth mother holding me as I cried at the loss of her father, I became aware of a strange noise echoing in the background. It took me a moment to realize the sound wasn't coming from someone else—it was me. My own sobs were louder than I realized, and in that moment, I paused. I realized I had a choice: I could keep crying, or I could compose myself and let the service continue without disruption. I chose to pull myself together, and the service carried on.

After the funeral, the family all gathered at my grandparents' home. As we sat around talking, one of my cousins said something funny, and suddenly, we all burst out laughing. I was surprised by the joy and laughter that found its way into such a moment of grief. It was eye-opening to realize that even in deep sadness, I could experience joy. My emotions weren't fixed; I could shift how I felt in an instant. That realization stayed with me.

I also learned something else that day: life doesn't stop, even when your world feels like it's falling apart. As I grieved, I noticed the world around me kept moving, people left to go back to work or run errands. It was a stark reminder that no one else was experiencing pain the way I was. Life would continue, whether I was ready for it to or not. If I wanted a different life, one that wasn't defined by grief or sadness, I was going to have to pursue it. The choice to heal and move forward wasn't going to happen by chance; it had to be intentional.

Fear is an idol. It was for me. I didn't want to end up like my mother—single in her old age—or without a relationship with my children. But those very fears manifested. The thing I dreaded most became my reality. That's the nature of fear: it demands worship. It insists that you bow down to it, and inevitably, it shows up so you can confront it. All fears must be faced. It cannot be avoided. It might take a while to manifest but it will show up.

I learned this lesson early in life. When I was fifteen years old, I was watching TV with my aunt, who had an intense fear of snakes. As we watched a sitcom, out of nowhere, a diamondback rattlesnake appeared on the screen, coiled up. She screamed, jumped up, and ran out of the room. I sat there in shock, wondering how a snake had managed to appear at that exact moment. I didn't understand it then, but I see it clearly now: what you are afraid of, you attract. It may not happen immediately, but eventually, you'll face that fear.

This understanding clicked for me years later as I read the Bible repeatedly saying, "Do not be afraid." Why would God say that so often? Because fear is powerful—it shapes what we believe, what we pursue, and what we attract into our lives. God, in His infinite love, honors our will, even when our will is dictated by fear. He allows what we choose to manifest.

Was I afraid of being divorced or childless? Absolutely. I believe Julian had those fears too, so those fears had to be faced. The very things we think we can't handle are often what we're required to confront. It's how we learn the fallibility of the things we place our trust in—whether it's people, circumstances, or even ourselves.

We're tested in the areas where we think we are most vulnerable. That's how wisdom is born. Hindsight is 20/20, and as I look back, I see how my disobedience, desire for instant gratification, and fear of rejection paved the way for so many of the difficulties and disappointments in my marriage.

Fear is an idol that will always demand worship, but it's also a false god. It's only when we choose to trust in God's promises and let go of our fears that we can truly walk in the freedom and abundance He desires for us.

Now that I live as a single, childless woman, I've come to accept that healing is an ongoing journey. Pain and disappointment aren't things that can be quickly resolved, like crossing off a task on a to-do list. Healing takes time, and it requires continually looking inward to discover and address the unhealed roots buried deep in our hearts.

But those roots don't have to keep us stuck. Each day is an opportunity to experience life in a new way—different from how we thought it should be. I had to learn how to live life differently, and though it was challenging, it wasn't as devastating as what others have endured. I'm not the first woman to face divorce or childlessness, and I certainly won't be the last. As humans, we are incredibly resilient. The trials of life don't have to prevent us from moving forward; they can redirect us to a different, perhaps even better, path.

History is full of people who have faced far more dramatic challenges than most of us can comprehend, yet they persevered. That perspective reminds me to keep hope alive, even amid disappointment. While I would have loved to have my own biological children and family, I've realized that there are other ways to leave a legacy. Other ways to find fulfilment. Other ways to show the world my value and worth.

There are countless people I can impact and influence, and that's where my hope lies now. My legacy is no longer rooted in the shaky pedestals I once clung to but in a life spent tearing them down. It's about building something bigger than myself—something meaningful, enduring, and free from the false idols of the past. I'm not quite sure what they all are yet but I'm determined to find out.

Cheers to a life after all our idols have fallen.

Printed in Dunstable, United Kingdom